100 Must Do

BAHAMAS

Travel Guide

Table of Contents

TO TASTE

1 The ubiquitous conch

Price: $25 - $30

The conch is the most popular delicacy and a staple for every home, restaurant or even a roadside takeout stall in Bahamas. It is a type of sea snail fished from the shallows. The snail usually has a tough flesh and therefore tenderized by some TLC. The meat is usually pound and scored to marinate with some lime. The best places you can get some conch are roadside wooden shacks with good kitchens. The conch can also be found on the beachfronts.You can ask the locals the favourite variety type of tasty conch and have a taste of it.

2 Avant-garde sushi and sashimi

Price: $4 - $8

Enjoy one of the best meals like the Avant-garde sushi and sashimi with celebrity chef Nobu Matsuhisa's signature black cod at ultra-slick.

3 Bahama Mama

Price: $1 - $3

Bahama Mama is a fruity rum drink and among the best cocktails that is good for partying in the summer. Making a Bahama Mama at home is easy. Just like many tiki drinks, the drink is a popular cocktail prepared in many different ways. There should be two kinds of rum, a dose of pineapple, coffee, and some little coconut. The drink can be more basic with common ways of making it. It consists of different ingredients with some feel of lemon juice. The second one is a sweeter mix with grenadine and orange juice.

4 Goombay Smash

Price: $7 - $15

Smashes are drinks such as gin, whisky and rum with some mint and sugar. They are usually served in old fashion glasses. Goombay smash original version was first made in Green Turtle Cay. It is a popular drink all through Caribbean. You can opt for a pineapple, coconut or rum drink to enjoy and refresh yourself.

5 Sky Juice

Price: $16

A true Bahamian Sky Juice requires gin, a drink which was quite cheap to afford for the poor dating many years back. Sky juice which is also referred to as Gully Wash became staple in the Bahamian bars because of the ease of accessing its ingredients. Sky juice has a refreshing taste which makes it one of the most famous local drinks for both the visitors and locals.

6 Tortuga Rum Cake

Price: $1 per once

This is one dessert that is well known and famous. The dessert is made by different people from all over the world. To experience the goodness of the Tortuga Rum cake, then Bahamas should be the place to find one. This is because the cake is made encompassing the best flavours loved by most people all over the world. Have a visit to Bahamas and enjoy the sweetness of the Tortuga Rum Cake.

7 Fish soup

Price: $6 - $8

Enjoy the Bahamian fish chowder made from fish of any choice. The soup is mixed together with tomatoes, celery and cooking sherry among other ingredients. Some lime juice and dark rum is also added with other flavourings. Though it is increasingly becoming rare, some areas also do serve turtle soup.

8 Bahamian Johnnycake

Price: $5 - $10

The Johnny Cake does not fall or qualify to be in the realm of a dessert. It is comparable to bread although not typically the light and airy varieties. It has a texture like that of dense bread and slightly sweet cake. The cake is made from ingredients such as butter, sugar, baking powder, and flour among other major ingredients. It is baked traditionally in a large round pan until it turns to light brown. It is then sliced and served in wedges.

9 Lobster

Price: $7 - $10

During your stay in Bahamas, enjoy the tasty fresh lobster meal. The lobster is served traditionally with butter sauce. The meal is amongst the culinary highlights for the country.

10 The Bahamian Souse

Price: $7 - $10

It is a traditional Bahamian stew. The famous of the souse is the one made using chicken wings. The Souse is cooked with vegetables such as onion, pepper, potatoes and carrots

For a good sauce, quality ingredients and spices are used in flavouring the soup. The major ingredients used are bay, lime and allspice.

Historical and Cultural Sights

Bahamas has one of the best and stunning cultural and historical sights.

11 Fort Montagu

Location: Fort Montagu, E Bay St

Open hours: 9 am – 5 pm (Wed – Sat)

Price: free

Being the remaining oldest strongholds of Nassau, Fort Montagu was built in 1741 to guard the Eastern part of the Nassau Harbour. There is a park surrounding the Fort Montagu.

12 Bahamas Historical Society Museum

Location: Shirley St, Nassau

Open hours: 10 am - 4 pm (Mon- Fri)

Price: $0.5 - $1

It is the major museum owned by the Bahamas Historical Society. The museum consists of a variety of documents and artefact collection. The collections have span for more and more years of the history of Bahamas. At this museum, the featured collections you can discover if you happen to make a visit here include stone slabs, petroglyphs, coat of arms and the island's Declaration of Independence. Though the place may not have many tourists visiting, you will definitely find a good number of hotels to choose from and enable your accessibility in visiting this historical place.

13 Nassau Public Library

Location: Shirley St, Nassau

Open hours: 10 am – 8 pm (Mon - Thur), 10 am – 5 pm (Fri), 10 am – 4 pm (Sat)

Price: free

Nassau Public Library is the oldest government building that was built in 1797. The building initially served as a jail in the 1800s. What used to be cells are now full of books and periodicals. This is the best place for chilling and enjoying the historical thrills. The library therefore remains a historical and reference library being the home of the history of Bahamas since the colonial times to date. Since the library's conversion from a prison to a reading place, there has been a considerable increase in the number of services provided. There has also been technological advancements since then.

14 Lucayan National Park

Location: The Bahamas

Open hours: 8:30 am- 4:30 pm

Price: $5

The national park lies on a 40-acre piece of land. Being the Grand Bahamas' finest treasure, it lies 25 miles east of Ranfurly Circle. It is well known for its underwater cave system that is amongst the longest ones in the world. Here, the visitors can check out for Burial Mound and Ben's Cave which are the two caves situated in the park. The remains of the earliest inhabitants were discovered here in the year 1986. The Lucayan National park is special since it is the habitat of all the six vegetation zones.

15 Watling's Castle

Location: Port Nelson, San Salvador

Open hours: always open

Price: free

Watling's Castle is a historical place with actual ruins of a building. In the 17th and early 18th century, the castle was initially a three-storey building with barns, slave quarters, boundary wall and kitchen. The greatness of Watling's Castle comes in due to the raw emotions that comes up when standing in the building's ruins. The emotions of being at the Watling's Castle ruins will take you back into a deep history of whatever occurred there. Similarly, it will allow you to experience whatever happened there.

16 Mt Alvernia Hermitage

Location: The Bahamas

Open hours: always open

Price: free

Mount Alvernia, which is also known as Como Hill, is the highest point in The Islands of The Bahamas. The mountain is 206 feet. It got its name Alvernia from Monsignor John Hawes who was a Roman Catholic priest. Monsignor John Hawes built the Hermitage on the peak the mountain in the year 1939.

17 Wyannie Malone Museum

Location: Queen's Hwy

Open hours: 10 am - 4 pm (Mon - Sat)

Price: $3 - $5

Wyannie Malone Museum has at least something for everyone. Visit the museum to explore the island heritage and gain experience to enrich your visits to Hope Town. You will be able to see history lively through the fascinating ship building displays, hurricanes and ship wreck displays. You will also get a glimpse of clothing and housewares that once existed long time ago. Bring the family to this small but engaging museum to lively see the historical times and also read more about how it came into existence.

18 Fort Fincastle

Location: Bennet's Hill, Prison Lane, Nassau

Open hours: Mon - Fri

Price: $1.20

The fort was built in 1793. It lies atop Bennet's Hill. Fort Fincastle was built to protect the any external threats to those living in Nassau. It is a site that sits alongside Queen's Staircase which is a popular and famous landmark. The historic fort gives the visitors some history about how life sounded like in the American Revolution. It also gives history on how the Great Britain moved on and protected its assets afterwards.

19 National Art Gallery of the Bahamas

Location: Nassau

Open hours: 10 am – 5 pm (Tue- Fri)

Price: $5 - $10

The creativity from the Bahamian community is that amazing. The Bahamians have created some art for displaying and showcasing their history, tough life and their positive side of life. This National Art Gallery has some art made from renowned artists on many of its islands. It is a fabulous place to spend some time especially during a rainy day. The price here is considerable, that is, $10 for adults and nil fees for the kids.

20 Pirates of Nassau Museum

Location: Nassau

Open hours: 8:30 am – 5:30 pm (Mon – Fri)

Price: $15

The most famous pirates in the world built Nassau museum and made Nassau a habitat back in the 1700s. This museum helps you check out how life was for these pirates. It has many things of treasure and artefacts from long time ago. Other displays have also been set up to give correct looks concerning the pirates' life. The charges here run from $13 for adults and $6.5 for the kids.

21 Queen's Staircase

Location: Elisabeth Ave, Nassau

Open hours: Mon - Sun

Price: free

Commonly referred to the 66 steps, the Queens Staircase is a key landmark that is situated in Nassau in the Fort Fincastle Historic Complex. The staircase was formed from solid limestone rock by slaves. This happened in the years 1973 and 1974. Queens Staircase is said to provide a direct route to Nassau City from Fort Fincastle. The steps were later on named after Queen Victoria who had led Britain for a period of 64 years. This is a perfect opportunity for taking photos and enjoying your moments.

22 Pompey Museum

Location: 2 W Bay St, Nassau

Open hours: 9:30 am - 4:30 pm (Mon – Sat)

Price: $1 - $2

The museum was named after the Bahamian slave who led a rebellion that was unsuccessful. The spare but moving museum takes you back to the harrowing 'Middle Passage' slave voyages. Pompey Museum is located in a former auction site for the slaves. The museum is always open for you every Monday, Wednesday and Friday. The charges here are $3 for adults, $1 for kids and $2 for the seniors.

23 Blackbeard's Tower

Location: Nassau, New Providence Island

Open hours: 9 am - 3 pm (Tue- Wed)

Price: $1 - $3

This semi-derelict tower is a historical building that is situated few miles to the east of Fort Montagu. The Blackbeard's Tower was built by Edward Tech also known as the dreaded

24 Versailles Gardens

Location: Paradise Island Dr, Nassau

Open hours: 9:00 am - 6:30 pm (Tue- Sat)

Price: free

Versailles Gardens is a hushed intimate garden found on the Paradise Island. It is a formal landscape that is lined with sculptures depicting historic men such as Hercules and Franklin D Roosevelt throughout the ages. The biggest photo in the garden is the Cloister which was built by Augustinian monks. The gardens are a popular wedding spot. Visit the gardens to have a feel of the best moments ever.

25 St Augustine's Monastery

Location: Nassau, New Providence Island

Open hours: 8 am - 5 pm (Mon – Fri)

Price: free

St Augustine's Monastery was designed by Father Jerome. The historic building dates back to 1947 and is still being used by the Benedictine monks. The monks give guided tours in the gardens that give a picture of the fascinating monastic life. There is also a college that is run by monks in this specific place.

Festivals Calendar

26 The annual Bahamian Music and Heritage Festival

The Bahamian Music and Heritage Festival is a very good time to enjoy with the family as a whole. It takes place every *March* of every year. There are a lot of activities for adults and kids. The activities run from singing, reading poetry and telling stories. There are contest demonstrations such as peeling onions and sugarcane. There is also stating of the history of Bahamas during this festivals. During the weekend the main occasions are the launch of gospel explosion. There is also a lineup of renowned and famous performers, both local and visiting. The attendees are entertained by local and national secular and gospel musicians.

27 Bahamas National Trust Art & Wine Festival

This is the festival where the local vendors display and expose their talents to buyers looking for high-quality products. The festival mainly features the art and culture of Harbour Island. It also involves different artists from different islands of Bahamas. For the followers of art collections and fine wine, then attend such festivals every *October*, which is the month they are held.

28 Bahamas International Film Festival

The Bahamas International Film Festival showcases a variety of foreign and local indie films in **December**. The festival provides special programs for educating the people, various cultural experiences and venturing into the field of cinema in the past, present and the future. Despite showcasing the films, the culture has been spread to very many film professionals all over the world.

29 Grand Turk Game Fishing Tournament

The Game fishing event is always held at the end of ***July*** and early ***August***. The tournament majors in fishing. You can choose to compete with other fishermen in fishing and presents are given in consideration of the largest fish caught and the greatness of the fish's weight.

An award of $100,000 US present is given to the fisherman who manages to catch 437 and above pounds Blue Marlin. Visit Bahamas in July and August to participate and enjoy the tournament.

30 Christmas tree Lighting Ceremony

The ceremony is always held by Grand Turk every ***mid-December*** of every year. This is a festive season for having fun and celebrating the birth of Jesus. Christmas is a symbol of hope and a suitable time to thank God for his greatest gift to all. The Christmas Tree Lighting Ceremony is attended by thousands of people every year. The attendees of the ceremony are always entertained by soothing music and melodious voices. The ceremony hosts different sorts of people ranging from children, adults, locals and visitors from outside Bahamas. This makes Bahamas a magical place to be and enjoy.

Top 14 Beaches

When one hears of Nassau, then water and beaches should be the very first thing to think of. The place hosts some of the best beaches in the world. Therefore, if you are looking towards relaxing, enjoying on the sand and swimming, then the best place to be is automatically here.

The following are the beaches that are actually recommended for any traveler who needs to explore pleasure to the fullest:

31 Pig beach

Location: Pig Island

The Pig Island on the Big Major Cay is a habitat for swimming pigs. The island is known for the Exuma pigs. The beach has warm sand with crystal-blue waters and a Caribbean breeze that originates from the rustling palm trees around it. You can opt to personally swim with the cute and pink pigs that float in the Caribbean Sea under the sun. The Pig Beach is one of the visited beaches by tourists.

32 Xanadu Beach

Location: Freeport

Xanadu beach is located far off from Port Lucaya and it is dominated by the decaying Xanadu Beach. For an easy afternoon trip, it can be considered close enough despite being far from Port Lucaya. Sands on this beach are powdery with warm and blue water. Take a cab or drive to Xanadu beach a few miles to the west of Port Lucaya and enjoy what the beach has for you.

33 William's Town Beach

Location: Williams Town, Freeport

The beach is also famously known as the Islands Sea Beach. It is located directly west of Lucaya and Silver Point Beaches with a separation of a concrete channel. The narrow sand-stripped beach is not only known for its beauty but also its enjoyable nightlife. When dark comes in, the locals and tourist park into the beachfront bars such as the Two-Dollar Bar to take some drink.

34 Gold Rock Beach

Location: Lucayan National Park

It is one of the marvelous beaches mainly having a large number of sea birds and raccoons.

It is a part of Lucayan National Park consisting of a stretch of golden sand. It is termed the most beautiful beach of the island, which is actually an indisputable fact. On arriving at this beautiful place, you can pay some entrance fee of about $3 and enjoy hiking the short trail down the stretch of golden sand. Suppose you don't have a way to get to the Gold Rock Beach, then tour operators in town are there for you offering some group excursions.

35 Pretty Molly Beach

Location: Sea Horse Road, Freeport

Despite the sorrowful origin of its name, Pretty Molly Beach is one of the best beaches on the island. The name originated when a slave had to kill herself after walking into the waves past the beach. The beauty of these shore is quite compelling for one to visit it and enjoy the waters.

36 Cable Beach

Location: Nassau

Possibly the best-renowned beach in Nassau, it is situated on the northern shore of New Providence. Cable beach is close to the cruise port with some hotels such as Sheraton nearby. This is the beach where crowds of people will always converge.

The quality of the sand is so good with welcoming shallow waters. Close to the Cable beach are many precious bars from where you can actually grab a drink and enjoy as you catch a tan.

37 Cabbage Beach

Location: Nassau, New Providence Island

Cabbage beach is situated on the Paradise land, but then it doesn't extend to be part of Atlantis Resort. The goodness with the beach compared to other beaches such as Cable beach is that it's not that overcrowded. Although, it's actually a good beach, the waters can be rough and violent at times. But then the beach is actually a fabulous place to enjoy the day because there are some drinks that come around from time to time.

38 Junkanoo Beach

Location: W Bay St, Nassau

While Cable beach lies in the western part of the cruise port, Junkanoo Beach lies to the east.

This is just on the way to the Paradise Island. The beach is well-renown among the locals who will always hang out, grill and enjoy life. The gentle sheltered waters here will always motivate you with a stunning blue colour. This overlooked gem is such a good place to enjoy the rest of your day.

39 Montagu Beach

Location: Nassau

Montagu Beach is another gem situated on the east of New Providence. The waters are ideal for wading in the more relaxed atmosphere. The relaxed atmosphere here will definitely allow you to rest, meditate upon your life and even take a nap if tired. You can carry your own drinks to this fabulous place since drinks are not actually offered here.

40 Ben Bay Beach

Location: The Bahamas

Located 10 miles from the North of Eleuthera International Airport, the well-protected Ben Bay Beach has an almost perfectly snorkeling and calm waters.

41 Pink Sands Beach

Location: Isla Harbour

Pink Sands Beach is a fine Harbour Island beach. The sand at this fine beach really glows a pink light shade. This comes about of the smoothly pulverized coral.

42 Lighthouse Beach

Location: The Bahamas

A drive down the almost impossible 3-mile road will lead you to a dazzling crescent of sand which is in the Lighthouse Beach. While here, you can be able to explore the old lighthouse. On the other side of the hill is the beach which is a stretch of some coral-pink sand with chalky white cliffs and a thick white forest.

The beach is calmer and shallow compared to other Atlantic side beaches. Sometimes, the beach might have a strong undertow and therefore the need to be careful while exploring it.

43 Club Med Beach

Location: The Bahamas

Club Med Beach is a beautiful and prettiest beach surrounded by a finely curving shore. It is located on the left of Quality Inn Cigatoo along the Atlantic on Haynes Ave.

44 Ten Bay Beach

Location: The Bahamas

It is a quiet beach shaded with palm alcove. Ten Bay Beach is bordered by Savannah Sound on the Caribbean side. It is one of the greatest beaches for beachcombing with shallows that trap small conch shells and starfish. To get to this place, simply take a 3.5-mile drive past Palmetto Point junction.

Islands

45 Harbour Island

The Island has pink sandy beaches. It is a perfect getaway for any vacationer. You can walk around the lanes of the old town to enjoy watching beautiful sceneries and later on swim in the clear water whilst watching the spectacular sun setting in the horizon.

46 Windermere Island

The island has snazzy homes that reflect its status as one of the exclusive hideaways for the famous and rich. It has the most fashionable resorts such as the Windermere Island Club.

47 Berry Islands

It is the most popular destination for the yachties. The island has no tourism infrastructure and attracts some precious vacationers. This is an ideal place to spend your long day from one secluded cay to another. There are also other activities such as bone fishing, beachcombing, and snorkelling in isolated coves. The island make up to 12 square miles of the land.

48 Crooked Island

It is a beautiful island with beaches, lakes and bisected tidal inlets. Crooked Island has pretty natural charm as a great place to sit, relax and enjoy. The island is mostly covered by members of the Seventh Day Adventist. Therefore, on Fridays evenings and Saturday mornings the island comes to a standstill because of the Seventh-Day-Adventists.

49 Long Island

Long Island is one of the most attractive islands that has various attraction sites such as the lush greenery, sky-blue Gothic churches, plantation ruins and others. It has also magnificent beaches, bays and blue holes. The inhabitants of this island mainly plant bananas, corn, vegetables and pineapples. This paradise is full of untapped precious things and therefore if you happen to pay a visit here, then it turns out to be the place that makes your day.

50 North Long Island

Explore the Columbus memorial, vivid seas where you will enjoy snorkelling boats and also diving in the sea. It is also important to carry with you insect spray for mosquitoes and sand flies.

All these will be enjoyed in the Northern part of the island.

51 Acklins Island

It is separated by a shallow passage from the Crooked Island. It has some excellent bone fishing lodges scrub forest and other attraction sites. The main settlement here is the Spring Point which is midway down the west coast. Many people here earn from fishing and beating the Cascarilla bark which is an important ingredient for Campari.

52 Caicos Islands

It is the main island of the nation that forms the fan of all the islands. The island is separated into South Caicos, Providenciales, Middle Caicos, North Caicos, East Caicos and West Caicos. It has numerous deserted and inhabited tiny islands. A lot of people all over the world visit the island to spend their holiday.

53 Cat Island

It is a fascinating destination to stop at since the heart of the Bahamian traditional African Culture lies here. The island is blessed with Como Hill which has a height of about 206 feet, some rolling hills and an enjoyable atmospheric hermitage. The north shore has dramatic beaches and dramatic cliffs.

54 Paradise Island

The island has almost everything you deserve to experience while in Bahamas. These ranges from golf club, casino, waterpark and marine parks. The place has well-maintained gardens such as the Versailles and French Cloister.

BARs & CLUBs

55 Leeward Yacht Club

Location: Green Turtle Cay

It is located on the Green Turtle Cay in Abaco. The marina will enable you to access sailboat, yachts and powerboats easily. To access the club, you just have to simply walk to the quaint and historical town of New Plymouth. The club provides various services such as cycling, paddle boarding, deep sea diving and kayaking among others. In need of an out island experience full of concierge amenities? Then Leeward Yacht Club is here for you.

56 Bacardi Store & Bar Lounge

Location: Nassau New Providence Island

Bacardi Store & Bar Lounge is another place reserved for the cruisers. The bar is situated right by the port. It has great atmospheric conditions that will favor you while at the bar.

57 Havana Cay Cigar Bar

Location: Freeport

A beamed ceiling and wrought iron light fixtures create an Old World ambience at this clubby cigar bar, in the 'Manor House' lobby of the Radisson Our Lucaya.

58 Sharkeez Tiki Bar

Location: Woodes Rodgers Walk, Nassau

The bar is situated off Woodes Rogers Walk with a very small distance from Saunders Beach.Sharkeez Tiki is a good bar to visit and enjoy your time sipping a drink of your own choice. The bar has a rocking and relaxed atmosphere where you can take daiquiris, Bahama Mama's and hurricanes accompanied by some cool soothing music.

59 Daiquiri Shack

Location: Nassau

Daiquiri Shack is located right off Cable beach and this is where you can get some drink suppose Bahamas gets hotter. Here, you will find drinks of your choice to carry them on over at your own wish. Drinks at this bar are strong with reasonable and affordable prices. Everything here is refreshing and cold and therefore the need check in Daiquiri Shark to enjoy your most favorite drinks.

60 Lizard Bar & Grill

Location: Nassau

Lizard Bar and Grill is an outdoor bar, which serves a large number of customers with international foods such as ahi tuna burgers and shrimp kebabs among other delicious foods.

61 Aura

Location: Paradise Island

The club was designed for recreation to get rid of the exclusive feeling that may lack in any trendy nightclub in New York. This is where the DJs spin like the couture-clad partiers. The operation time runs from 9:30 pm to 4 am on every Thursday and Saturday of the week. Aura is the club where the young and upcoming celebrities almost get wild on their first visit for its astonishing and special way of partying. Charges here always vary and therefore the need of taking chance to grab the cheapest and affordable promotional pass.

62 Hammerhead Bar & Grill Bar

Location: Nassau, New Providence Island

This funky little bar is located between the two Paradise Island Bridges. It offers live music over the weekends has all kinds of people visiting the bar. This ranges from the locals, Spring Beakers and the yachties.

63 Club Waterloo

Location: E Bay St, Nassau

It is an old mansion on the lakeside located near Fort Montagu. It has different outdoor and indoor dance floors and some multiple bars. Club Waterloo has at least everything you can think of enjoying provided that your age bracket ranges from 18 to 25. The music played in this club ranges from calypso to techno with some heavy emphasis on beats that are booty-shaking.

The ladies night is held on every Thursday night with weekends having some live bands.

64 Plato's Lounge

Location: Paradise Island

Located inside Atlantis, Plato's Lounge first-rated bar by all the visitors or tourists. Plato's lounge offers high quality though expensive drinks which will give you the treat you would wish to have. Plato Lounge is not only a party spot but also a place to explore a variety of drinks and activities.

65 Elvina's bar

Location: Queen's Hwy

Experience legendary nights every Tuesday and Friday at the old-school party shack Elvina's bar. It is just around the bend from town. The place is thronged by different visiting musicians and locals who entertain in the place.

66 Shenanigan's Irish Pub

Location: Bay St, Nassau

If you're craving a Guinness or a plate of bangers and mash, this dimly lit Irish pub is your place. Daily happy hours pack in the (mostly foreign) crowds.

67 Cafe Matisse

Location: Nassau

Café Matisse is one of the best points to stop at and enjoy an experience of the best foods ever. It is a restaurant that is situated by the cruise port. The unusualness with this restaurant is that you will be able to find the most amazing dishes such as cracked lobster. Café Matisse is the most loved by the locals!

68 Seagulls Tiki Bar

Location: West Bay Street, Nassau, New Providence Island

The bar is situated on the Junkanoo Beach and provides quality services and reasonable prices of each and every drink you would wish to have. Seagulls Tiki Bar gives a special offer of a three short and three beer for 10 dollars. This will actually keep one feeling right for the long haul.

Outdoor Adventures and Nature

69 Walker's Cay National Park

To automatically fall in love with nature, you simply have to pay a visit to the Walker's Cay National Park. It is a popular nature preserve that is located in Walkers Cay found to the northwest of Bahamas. The park has very clear water with which you can be able to see to about 100 feet deep. The major reason for the clarity of the water is that the Walker's Cay lies outside the sea's major trade lines.

70 Ardastra Gardens

It is a zoo and conservation center. Ardastra Gardens is a fantastic place to visit since it has amazing wildlife to much with its beautiful gardens. The animals and birds found in this zoo include parrots, pigs, rabbits, iguanas and many others. An assortment of vibrant tropical plants is featured here hence a greater opportunity for photo taking. Tickets in this place are $19 for adults and $9 for the kids.

71 Aquaventure

It is the largest water park in the Caribbean lying on a 141-acre piece of land with pools and water rides. The aquatic place consists of Atlantic-themed towers, long river ride with rolling rapids and many swimming areas among other interesting features. Aquaventure is a perfect environment for all those who are on vacation. It simply delivers an aqua adventure like no other.

72 Abaco National Park

The national park was developed in 1994 and covers an area of about 32 square miles. It was established for the purpose of protection of the endangered species of Bahamas parrot. Abaco National Park has a variety of parrots and some wild pigs with some stunning orchids. Apart from that, there is also a wide cave system to explore, with lonesome beaches and sceneries like no other along the Atlantic shore. The area is also covered by 5000 acres of pine forest which is the main home for the Bahama Parrot.

73 Preacher's Cave

It is a very large cave situated 2 miles to the east of the Jean's Bay. It was founded in 1648 and termed as the place where the Eleutheran Adventurers secured shelter and constructed an altar from where they prayed in order to be rescued. In front of the cave is one of the several glorious beaches along the north coast. Locating the cave might be somehow tricky. Have a visit to the cave and catch a glimpse of some of the remnants of the belongings the Adventurers used during their time.

74 Blue Lagoon

The lagoon is a stretch of sugar white sand that is covered by coconut palms and surrounded by a turquoise lagoon and an excellent rain forest. The lagoon is also referred to as Salt Cay. The island here is developed with nature trails, good beaches and volleyball courts hence being the most popular and family-friendly place. You can opt to sign up to enjoy various sports such as kayaking, paddle boating at an affordable price. Carry your family here to enjoy a long fun day in the sun.

75 Flaming flamingos

The flamingos are restricted to Great Inagua. Many of these birds inhabit Lake Rosa, which a long lake is covering up to 12 miles in the Bahamas National Trust Park. The birds exist in great flocks in the park especially in the period ranging from November to July. The mating season of the birds occurs in December and January and nesting season is as from February to April.

76 Jojo

This is a bottle-nosed dolphin, which is 7 feet and found in Provo and North Caicos. On its first appearance, the dolphin seemed to be shy and had limited interaction with the humans through playing in bow waves of boats. Visit Bahamas and enjoy playing with the dolphin that is playful with a lot of companionship.

77 Mangrove Cay

Mangrove Cay is the most rural and isolated chunk of Andros. It has not made more changes since the first century. The island has Moxey Town which has a number of houses that overlook the Middle Bight.

78 Green Turtle Cay

It is found on the far north of the four Loyalist cays. It has a number of activities to do and explore.

It is ideal for getaways and family vacations particularly those who are vacationers. The Green Turtle Cay is a popular destination as for wedding venues. It is also a kick-off point for the fishing tournament season. It is an inspiration to many who visit it and end up writing about the good and enjoyable encounters they experienced during their visit to this Cay.

79 Loyalist Memorial Sculpture Garden

It is located close to Albert Lowe Museum in Green Turtle Cay. It was built through fundraising by New Plymouth Historical Society. It is a monumental tribute for the historians who had a major role in the Abacos history. It has 24 busts of famous Bahamians that surround bronze sculptures of two girls. This represent a new beginning in the Bahamas for the many of Loyalists in the American Revolution.

80 Hatchet Bay Cave

This is a half-mile long cave system. The cave descends into a vertical hole with chambers that have charcoal signatures that have existed ever since the mid-19th century. Inside the caves are leaf-nosed bats, which are harmless. They reside within the cave on stalactites and stalagmites. Visit and explore the cave system, which is too dark hence, the need of carrying with you a flashlight.

81 Mount Olympus and Memory Rock

The two sites, Mount Olympus and Memory Rock, are ranked amongst the most spectacular sites. The sites are located far from the island on the eastern edge of Gulf Stream. Memory Rock is a fantastic wall dive that sports a number of sponges, gorgonians and corals. Mount Olympus on the other side is an atmospheric site that features valleys, gullies and prominent mountain-like coral boulders.

82 Little Stirrup Cay

The cay is also known as the CoCo Cay. It offers the best things a vacationer can do while in Bahamas. There are varieties of water sports that take place here. Despite enjoying the water sports, you can also decide to laze on the beautiful white sandy beach. Then take a refreshing tropical drink with the cool ocean breeze soothing you.

83 Ardastra Gardens & Zoo

Ardastra Gardens & Zoo is specifically here for you if you are a fun of spending time with different kinds of animals. The zoo is situated downtown Nassau which is a shorter drive when going to see the beautiful animals. This is a family friendly garden and zoo. That is, the place is great for spending time with the family. You will enjoy seeing beautiful pink flamingoes and chatty parrots here.

84 Harrold and Wilson Ponds

The Harrold and Wilson Ponds lying on 250 acres of land is situated in the South Central New Providence. It has more than 100 species of avian, which include the egrets, cormorants and ibises among others. There is an ecotourism and exceptional educational site that adds to the parks beauty.

85 Exuma Cays Land & Sea Park

This is an ideal park with all kinds of fish and marine life. The park has protected islands of about 175 miles. It was founded in 1958. Surprisingly, there is no any kind of fishing and collection that takes place in this park. The park extends 22 miles from Wax Cay Cut up to Conch Cut and Fowl Cay. It has all sorts of seabirds and land animals.

86 Moriah Harbour Cay National Park

The park lies on 13,440 acres of land. It has mangrove creeks, beaches and sand dunes among other tourist attraction sites. It has a variety of birds to enjoy watching. Mangroves also exist in the park where conch, crabs and gray snappers make it a habitat. The Moriah Harbour Cay is an example of coastal area that is of additional importance to the park system.

87 Inagua National Park

It lies on 183, 740 acres of land covering an area of 287 square miles of the Great Inagua Island. The park is the largest breeding place for West Indian flamingoes. It is a home for birds such as the West Indian Whistling Ducks, Brown Pelicans and White Cheeked Pintails. Have a visit to the park and enjoy the greatest bird watching experience.

88 Great Harbour Cay

It is the major center of all the islands. This is where most islanders will live and at the same time where visitors will look for lodgings, food and company. It is built on a narrow channel to the south of the island's main settlement. The main attraction on the island is the white sand beach, which is 8 miles long. The beach lies along the eastern shore with warm shallows. There are other attractions such as Sugar Beach and the Bay Harbour Bay.

89 Mystery Cave

It is a deep blue hole situated on the Atlantic side with some living stomatolite reefs. The major reef is a living fossil which is believed to have existed in the last 3 ½ million years ago.

Some Interesting Hotels

90 Sandals Royal Bahamian Resort

It is amongst the most popular, luxurious, and all-inclusive resort brands in the world. This is the place you can spend your money on drinks and many activities. You will also be able to get good rooms with brilliant first-rate service from the service providers.

91 Orange Hill Beach Inn

The spotty Orange Hill Beach Inn will charge you almost $100 for every night. It is a precious and pretty inn located close to the airport. It is one a somehow luxurious inn with clean rooms and spacious beds. The meals here are tasty and delicious.

92 Quality Inn Junkanoo Beach

The hotels located on Junkanoo Beach with spacious rooms charging about $100 in a single night. Though the rooms are somehow outdated than those of Orange Hill Beach in, there are more acceptable especially if you are looking for a budget hotel on the beach.

93 Courtyard Nassau Downtown

The hotel charges $160 dollars for every night spent. A famous hotel provides good value for money. It is located some distance away from the British Colonial Hilton. The rooms here are so nice with recent renovations. Services provided by the employees are improved making this Courtyard a decent place to be.

94 Sunset Resort Bahamas

It is located at Junkanoo Beach with a history of recent renovations. It is one of the favourite places to visit. Rooms here are clean and this is the place you will have access to a private pool that is reserved for guests in the hotel. The hotel makes travelling to Cable beach much enjoyable. Sunset Resort charges $150 for every night spent.

95 Baha Mar Resort

The resort opened its doors recently after uncertainties and many years of delays. Baha Mar Resort is so stunning through offering of many beach, hotel and casino activities. Grand Hyatt manages it. A trip to this special hotel is a once in a lifetime event.

Original Local and Authentic Souvenirs

96 Straw Baskets, Bags & Hats

Price: $18 - $25

This are a must-have gift that you should not miss to buy from Nassau Paradise Island. The baskets and bags were used to carry caught fish and fruits. They are made from palm and sisal plants that are dried. They are woven together to form the baskets, bags and huts. Get yourself one or more of this souvenirs as a remembrance of your stay in Bahamas.

97 Wooden Carvings

Price: $33 - $40

There are a perfect choice for art lovers. The carvings are carved using a wooden carving knife. Choose all the wooden carvings that satisfy you ranging from exotic birds, wooden tropical fish and tribal mask. Pick a wood carving of your choice and keep in as a remembrance of you holiday in Bahamas.

98 Conch Shell Jewelry

Prices: $5 - $30

Since Conch is a national food in Bahamas, there is the need of carrying home Conch Shell Jewelry. The shells are used in making chunky rings, necklaces and bracelets. Every kind of pink shell and white pearls of conch has its own casual elegance and distinct beauty.

99 Croix Hook Bracelet

Prices: $79 - $82

Visitors to Bahamas can get themselves some Croix Hook bracelets which are distinctive pieces of jewellery to carry home. You don't need to be a Crucian to own a Croix Hook Bracelet. It is designed and sold for many years by Sonja Ltd.

100 Batik Kitts

Prices: $15 - $40

They are reasonable fabrics, which are dyed colourfully. They range from pillow covers, dresses to wall hangings. The prices are also reasonable hence the need of considering going home with one or two. Carry some of them home since they are wallet-friendly. Keep them or use them for remembrance of your stay in Bahamas.